# TERRIFIC tees

## I CAN'T BELIEVE IT'S A T-SHIRT QUILT!

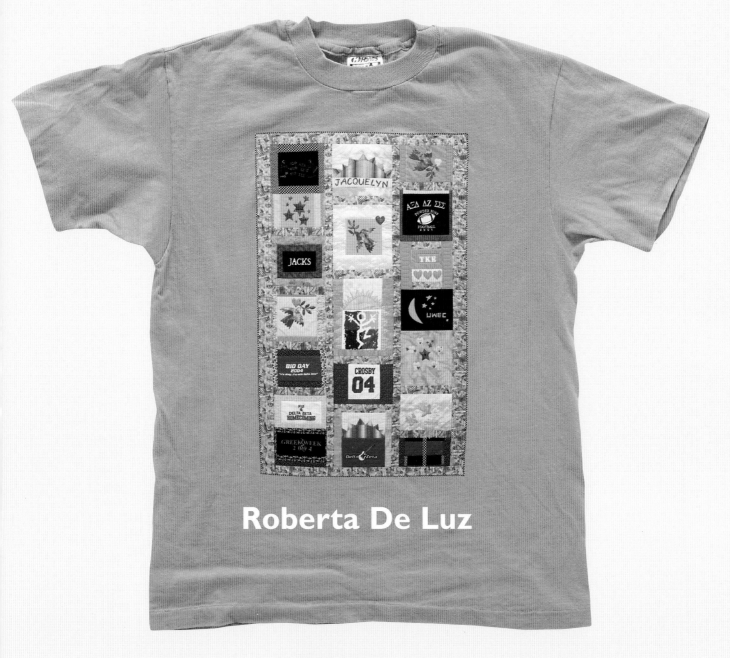

## Roberta De Luz

C&T PUBLISHING

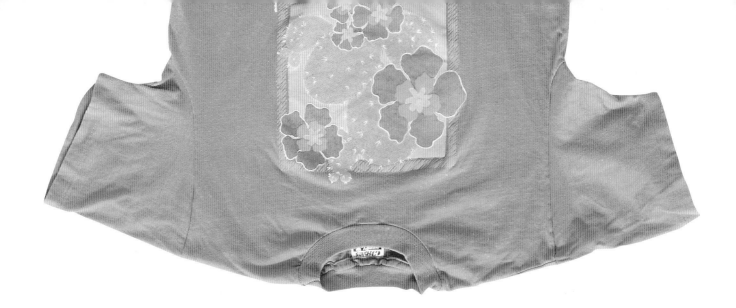

Text copyright © 2008 by Roberta De Luz

Artwork copyright © 2008 by C&T Publishing, Inc.

PUBLISHER: Amy Marson

EDITORIAL DIRECTOR: Gailen Runge

ACQUISITIONS EDITOR: Jan Grigsby

EDITOR: Liz Aneloski

TECHNICAL EDITORS: Helen Frost and Rebekah Genz

COPYEDITOR: Wordfirm Inc.

PROOFREADER: Stacy Chamness

COVER DESIGNER: Christina Jarumay

BOOK DESIGNER: Rose Sheifer-Wright

PRODUCTION COORDINATOR: Zinnia Heinzmann

ILLUSTRATOR: Tim Manibusan

Photography by Luke Mulks and Diane Pedersen of C&T Publishing unless otherwise noted

Published by C&T Publishing, Inc., P.O. Box 1456, Lafayette, CA 94549

Library of Congress Cataloging-in-Publication Data

DeLuz, Roberta.
  Terrific tees : I can't believe it's a T-shirt quilt! / Roberta DeLuz.
    p. cm.
  Includes bibliographical references and index.
  ISBN-13: 978-1-57120-460-8 (paper trade : alk. paper)
  ISBN-10: 1-57120-460-1 (paper trade : alk. paper)
  1. Patchwork--Patterns. 2. Quilting--Patterns. 3. T-shirts. I. Title.

TT835.D452 2008
746.46'041--dc22

                                        2007024740

Printed in China
10 9 8 7 6 5 4 3 2 1

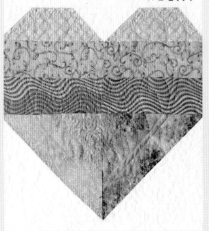

OUR REASON TO RELAY

## Dedication

This book is dedicated to my family. When I say *family*, I do not mean only people I am related to by blood, but the people I care most about.

First and foremost to the Hensley and Palsak families—Tony and Julie, Carrie and Kelly, George and Cindy, and all the boys, Luke, Josh, Matt, Jacob, Nick, and Andrew—without whom I could never have gotten here.

A big thank you to the members of my mini group, the Pickles, for their unwavering support. Whenever I needed feedback or an opinion, I could always count on them. A very special thank you to Clara Delgado, for all her help and encouragement, and to Karen Boutte, who kept me on task and answered her phone after 10 p.m.

To my son, Tony, and Angelina for making me a grandmother and giving me another reason to make quilts.

To my sweet Drew, who never knew what he started so many years ago on a Sunday afternoon.

# Contents

interests teams family pets

vintage hobbies career events

travel    concerts    school

favorite things    friends

# INTRODUCTION

Details of *Bay to Breakers* (quilt photo on page 15)

The purpose of this book is to change how you approach making a T-shirt quilt. Whether you are using team jerseys or tees commemorating a sporting event, rock concert, or school, the quilt will be unique and reflect the subject matter of the T-shirts.

A dear friend mentioned that she had many T-shirts from the Bay to Breakers race and asked if I could do something with them. Of course I could! What I didn't tell her was that I had no idea where to start. When she handed me all those wonderfully artistic shirts, I knew I needed to do something special. Knowing the beautiful setting of the race and what a great city San Francisco is, I started to think that this quilt deserved more than just a basic straight setting with some sashing. I wanted to make the quilt as memorable as the event. The quilt became a map of the race and a collection of snapshots of the city.

This book will help you find your way in making your quilt as special as your tees. Most of the quilts in this book use very traditional piecing and block patterns. The relationship between the subject of the tees and the quilt design is what makes these quilts so successful. Your tees will help you design your quilt.

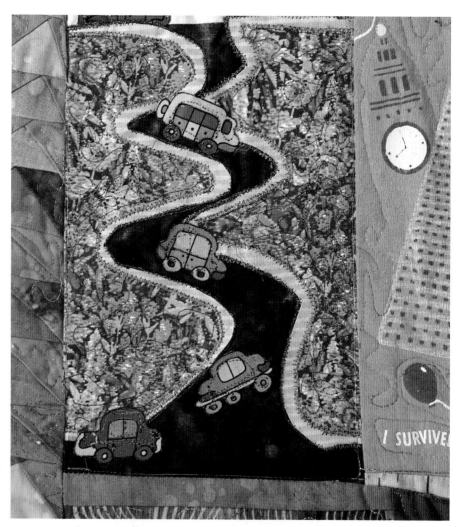

# GETTING STARTED

*Brown Avenue* (quilt photo on page 27)

*Let your mind run wild…*

## choosing a quilt design

Okay, you have a pile of tees. Now what? Are they from a sport, a school, maybe a local event? Let your mind run wild as you look at them. What is the connecting thread? How many tees do you have? What size are the designs? What size quilt do you want— wallhanging or bed size? The answers to these questions will help you design your quilt.

The theme for *Brown Avenue* is a quilt show. I had four tees. Traditional Sawtooth Stars are in some of the T-shirt motifs, so the shirts helped suggest the design.

*Go Bears* was probably the easiest of my T-shirt quilts to design. The Bear's Paw block was a natural for this quilt.

*Go Bears* (quilt photo on page 39)

*Relay for Life* (quilt photo on page 32)

*Relay for Life* took a different design path. As a fundraiser for the American Cancer Society, this walk is a very emotional event. The tees are mostly pinks and purples, which suggested hearts to me.

Some tees may not have a strong apparent connection, or they just might not work with the block approach. If that is your situation, give this a try. Take a step back, literally. Use a reducing glass to look at your collection of tees. You might notice a unifying color, theme, or shape that you didn't notice before.

Frame the tees to create uniformity, and fill in the spaces with simple blocks.

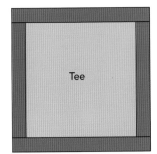

Frame the tees, if needed, to create a uniform size.

AMERICAN CANCER SOCIETY RELAY FOR LIFE ★ 2006
**WORKING TOGETHER TO SAVE LIVES**

Frame with a contrasting fabric as an accent.

AMERICAN CANCER SOCIETY RELAY FOR LIFE ★ 2006
**WORKING TOGETHER TO SAVE LIVES**

Frame with a blending fabric so the frame disappears.

The *Quick & Easy Block Tool* by C&T Publishing is a great resource for finding block possibilities. It includes cutting and piecing instructions for five block sizes.

Look at the quilts in this book or other books that contain quilt settings, such as *Smashing Sets* by Margaret Miller or *Great Sets* by Sharyn Craig. Maybe you'll get an idea that will get you started on *your* T-shirt quilt.

## fabric

For me, this is the easiest part of the whole process. I finally get to shop for fabric. Some collections of T-shirts will have a straight-forward color palette to guide the selections, but others are a little more challenging. When I'm choosing fabrics, I take my tees to the quilt store to help me pick the perfect fabrics. Gather fabrics that you think will work until you collect just the right balance of colors, prints, and values. Don't be afraid to use theme fabrics to reinforce the subject of your quilt.

# inspiration and ideas

Traditional quilt layouts are based on a grid. The number of tees you have will determine the number of grid sections in the layout. A good place to start is with a balanced layout in which the number of pieced blocks is approximately the same as the number of tees.

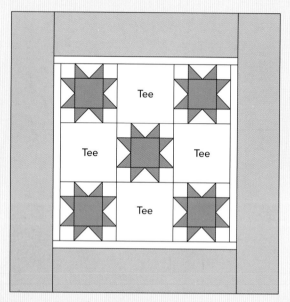

*Sawtooth Star*, 57″ × 57″, 12″ blocks, 12″ tees,
1½″ inner border, 9″ outer border

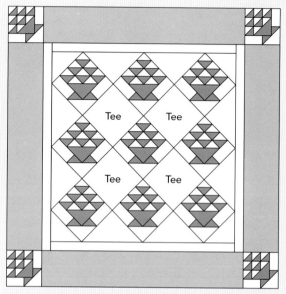

*Farmer's Market*, 60″ × 60″, 9½″ blocks, 9½″ tees,
2″ inner border, 8″ border and corner blocks

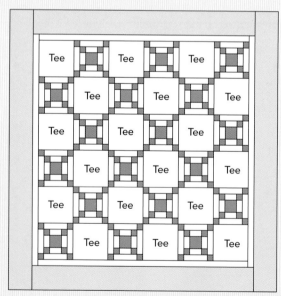

*Irish Chain*, 92″ × 92″, 12″ blocks, 12″ tees,
2″ inner border, 8″ outer border

*Square in Star*, 64″ × 64″, 12″ blocks with 4¼″ tees, 12″ tees,
6″ pieced star-point sashing, 2″ inner border, 6″ outer border

Another option is to use pieced sashing between the tees.

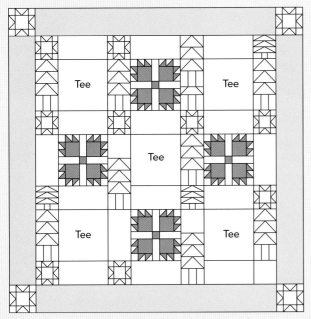

*Campin' in the Pines*, 63½" × 63½", 10½" blocks, 10½" tees,
5" pieced sashing, 6" borders and corners

Depending on the sizes of the designs on your tees, the layout may be smaller than you would like. If this is the case, increase the number of grid sections and add more pieced blocks until you have the size you want.

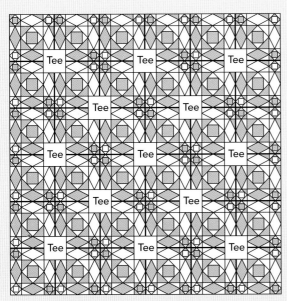

*Storm at Sea*, 72" × 72", 12" blocks, 6" tees

If your layout is too large, reduce the size of the grid sections and make the T-shirt design cover more than one grid section.

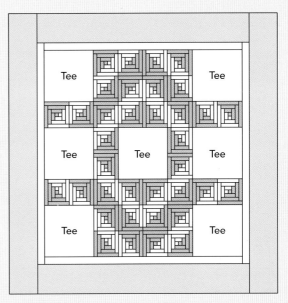

*Log Cabin*, 76" × 76", 7" blocks, 14" tees,
2" inner border, 8" outer border

This approach also works with a one-block layout, such as Trip Around the World.

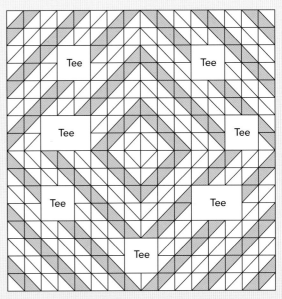

*Half-Square Trip Around the World*, 64" × 64",
4" half-square triangles, 8" × 8" and 12" × 8" tees

Sometimes a random setting is the way to go.

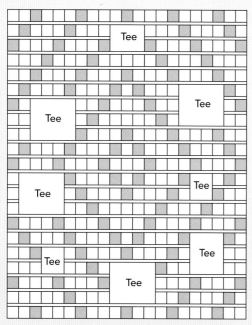

*Trip Around the World*; 42˝ × 52˝; 2˝ squares;
4˝ × 4½˝, 6˝ × 4½˝, 6˝ × 7˝, and 8˝ × 7˝ tees;
½˝ horizontal sashing

Be creative. Have fun.

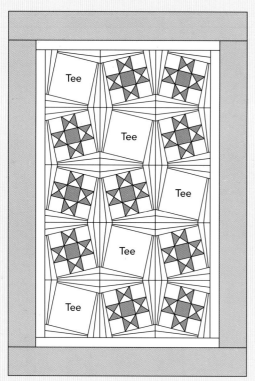

*Stars in Motion*, 52˝ × 76˝, 12˝ blocks, 9˝ tees,
2˝ inner border, 6˝ outer border

A center medallion setting might be just the thing for your quilt.

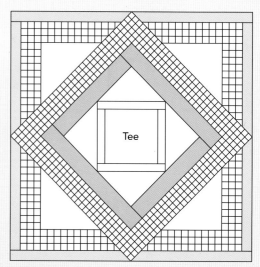

*One-Tee Wonder*, 45˝ × 45˝, $10\frac{3}{4}$˝ tee with 1˝ sashing,
9˝ half-square triangle setting triangles, 3˝ inner border,
4˝ checkerboard with 1˝ squares, $11\frac{1}{4}$˝ half-square
triangle setting triangles, $3\frac{3}{4}$˝ checkerboard with
$1\frac{1}{4}$˝ squares, 2˝ outer border

## Bay to Breakers

### BY ROBERTA DE LUZ

This was my first venture into T-shirt quilts. After I made this, I was hooked on the endless possibilities.

Nick's Quilt

BY ROBERTA DE LUZ

I made this quilt using a collection of my nephew Nick's team shirts. Many of them are a polyester blend, so it was important to keep the T-shirt motifs as small as possible to achieve a flat quilt.

Fighting Falcons

BY CATHY SHEA

This quilt captures the history of the football program at Freedom High School. The Football Mom
shirt highlights a program in which the moms suit up in their children's gear to learn the game.

Redwood Run

BY DEBBIE RODGERS

This quilt includes almost twenty years of Debbie's, her son's, and her husband's shirts. The quilt depicts the route over the river and through the redwoods to a large charity motorcycle rally.

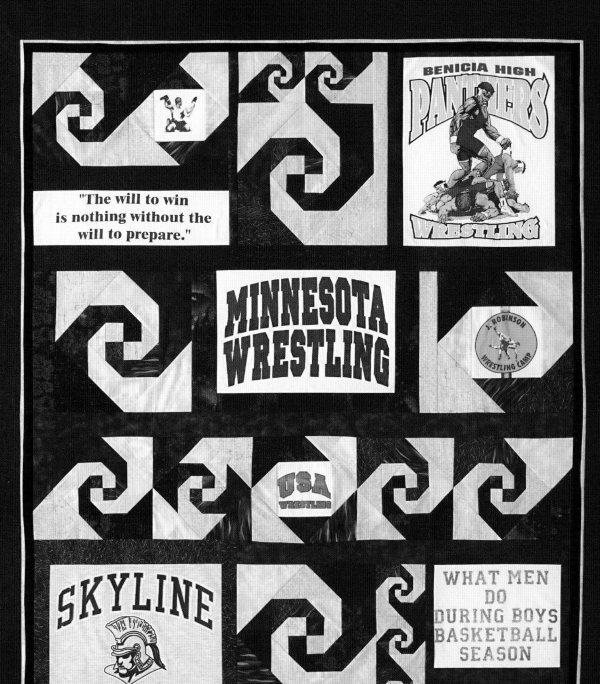

Take Down

BY JEANNE O'HAIR

The Snail's Trail interlocking block is a great accent for these wrestling shirts.
Notice how the strong colors unify the colors of the T-shirts.

Valerie's Campin' Quilt

BY CONNIE REGNER

Years of Girl Scouting are commemorated in this woodsy quilt.

100% Cute

BY KATE MCFAUL

Kate wanted something to commemorate her first son; the center of this quilt is stabilized onesies. The sashing, borders, and backing are the only cotton fabrics.

5, 6, 7, 8 . . .

**BY LESLIE BLACKIE**

The "5, 6, 7, 8" of her daughter's dance teachers came quickly to mind in
naming this quilt. The dancer silhouettes are appliquéd.

## Ride Around Corn County
### BY MELANIE REEVES-WICKLOW

This was Melanie's first quilt! The design of the bike
wheel and the camping motif are just delightful.

Jacks

BY SUSAN ANICH, QUILTED BY JUNE BELL

Original appliqués and folk art touches were used in this sorority-themed quilt.

# PREPARING THE TEES

**3**

In making quilts with tees, you are working with unruly knit fabrics of questionable fiber content. Regardless of what the label states (if you still have a label), knit fabric just moves very differently from the wonderful quilting cottons that we usually use.

So, our first task is to make these tees behave. This can be achieved with the help of our new best friend, nonwoven fusible interfacing.

Many tees are printed with heat-set inks, so when you iron the shirt the ink becomes a liquid again and can run or smear. The questionable fiber content can also cause problems, so use a nonstick-type pressing sheet.

**Tip** Before I start ironing, I mark the pressing sheet with "This side up." If you get ink on the pressing sheet and accidentally transfer it to your iron, you will be very unhappy.

*1.* Start with nice clean tees. Using a nonstick pressing sheet, press the tees.

Iron the tee using a pressing sheet.

*2.* Remove the iron and let the shirt cool for a few minutes so the ink sets and doesn't smear. Gently lift off the pressing sheet.

Gently lift off the pressing sheet.

*3.* Now comes the best part: cutting up the tees. Because you have already decided what size the motifs are going to be (pages 10–14), it's time to start working on the tees. Start by slicing up the sides. This gives you a nice flat surface to work with.

Cut up the sides.

*4.* Trim the motif to the finished block size plus 2˝. I like to use a 15˝ × 15˝ ruler.

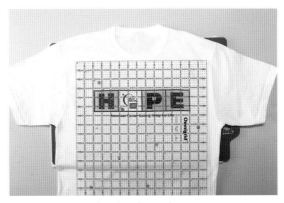

Place the ruler on the tee.

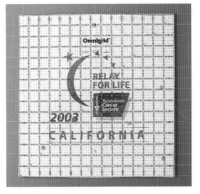

Trim.

5. Cut a piece of fusible interfacing about 1″ larger than the motif you just cut.

6. Place the fusible interfacing on a gridded ironing surface. If you don't have a commercially made one, mark your own grid with a permanent marker and a ruler. It isn't absolutely necessary, but it makes lining up the layers easier.

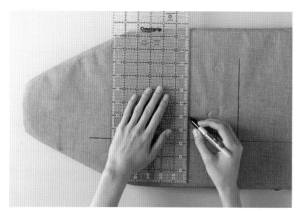

Mark a grid on the ironing surface.

7. Place the interfacing *adhesive side up* on the ironing surface. Place a pin in the corner if necessary to keep the interfacing from curling up.

8. Center the tee on top of the interfacing and place the pressing sheet on top.

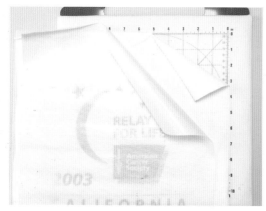

Layer the interfacing, tee, and pressing sheet.

9. Following the manufacturer's instructions, fuse the interfacing to the tee.

**Tip** Test the ironing time with scraps of the tee and interfacing. Make sure it fuses without any problems.

**Tip** Remove adhesive from the pressing sheet with a pastry scraper or old credit card.

Make sure you have no bubbles or loose spots that haven't fused. Unfused areas may form little pleats when you do the final quilting—which is not a major problem, just something to work around. It will quilt out, so don't worry!

So, now you have beautiful stabilized tees ready to be incorporated into beautiful quilts.

Prepared T-shirt block

When you are cutting the tee blocks for your quilt, add an extra $\frac{1}{8}$″ to the cut size. For example, for 12″ finished blocks, instead of cutting the tee blocks $12\frac{1}{2}$″ × $12\frac{1}{2}$″, cut them $12\frac{5}{8}$″ × $12\frac{5}{8}$″. Even with the interfacing, the tee blocks tend to curl up on the edges. Because they are also heavier than pieced blocks, adding an extra $\frac{1}{8}$″ to the cut size makes it easier to fit into the layout and gives you a little wiggle room.

**Tip** Use a large, leftover piece of tee as a test piece. Fuse it to interfacing and make a test sandwich with backing, batting, and the tee. Use it to test your quilting designs, batting, threads, and so on.

# BROWN AVENUE

*The very traditional subject matter, a quilt show, as well as some of the motifs featured on the shirts themselves, influenced this quilt. The sashing-style piecing of the large stars is the key to this quilt's design.*

Finished quilt: 78″ × 78″
**FINISHED BLOCK SIZES:**
Small Stars: 5″ × 5″
Medium Stars: 10″ × 10″

## materials

*Based on 42˝ fabric width.*

- Assorted plaids: 5 yards total for star blocks, feathers, and borders
- Black: 5¼ yards for background, sashing, and borders
- Green: ⅔ yard for vine
- Backing: 4¾ yards
- Batting: 82˝ × 82˝
- Binding: ¾ yard
- Lightweight fusible interfacing: 1¾ yards
- Fusible web: 3½ yards
- ¼˝ bias tape maker
- Template plastic
- Chalk marker

## cutting

Small Stars: 5˝ × 5˝; make 4.

| FABRIC | SIZE TO CUT | NUMBER TO CUT (PER BLOCK) |
|--------|-------------|---------------------------|
| Plaids | 1¾˝ × 1¾˝ | 8 |
| Plaids | 3˝ × 3˝ | 1 |
| Black | 1¾˝ × 1¾˝ | 4 |
| Black | 1¾˝ × 3˝ | 4 |

Medium Stars: 10˝ × 10˝; make 5.

| FABRIC | SIZE TO CUT | NUMBER TO CUT (PER BLOCK) |
|--------|-------------|---------------------------|
| Plaids | 3˝ × 3˝ | 8 |
| Plaids | 5½˝ × 5½˝ | 1 |
| Black | 3˝ × 3˝ | 4 |
| Black | 3˝ × 5½˝ | 4 |

Sashing

| FABRIC | SIZE TO CUT | NUMBER TO CUT (AS SHOWN) |
|--------|-------------|--------------------------|
| Plaids | 5½˝ × 5½˝ | 32 |
| Black | 10½˝ × 5½˝ | 24 |
| Black | 5½˝ × 5½˝ | 12 |

## construction

*Use a ¼˝ seam allowance.*

Prepare the shirts (pages 25–26) and trim to 10⅝˝ × 10⅝˝. Make 4.

### SAWTOOTH STARS

The same sequence is used for both sizes of stars.

Stitch.

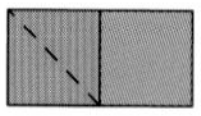

1. For the small star blocks, place a 1¾˝ plaid square on a 1¾˝ × 3˝ black rectangle. For the medium star blocks, place a 3˝ plaid square on a 3˝ × 5½˝ black rectangle. Draw a line and stitch from corner to corner.

Press.

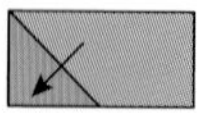

2. Trim the excess fabric and press.

3. Repeat for the other end of the black piece. Make 16 units for the small star blocks and 20 units for the medium star blocks.

Repeat.

4. Arrange the small units with the 3˝ plaid squares and 1¾˝ black squares. Arrange the medium units with the 5½˝ plaid squares and 3˝ black squares. Sew into rows. Press. Join the rows. Press. Make 4 small and 5 medium-sized stars.

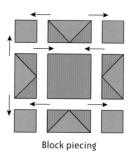
Block piecing

### LARGE SASHING STARS

Place a 5½˝ plaid square on a 10½˝ × 5½˝ black rectangle. Draw a line and stitch from corner to corner. Trim and press. Repeat for the other end.

Make 16.

## assembling the quilt top

Position and stitch the blocks, sashing pieces, and tees, referring to the quilt construction diagram. Press.

### INNER BORDER

1. Measure the distance around the edge of the quilt top.

2. From the plaids, cut strips 2½˝ wide by random 8˝–14˝ lengths. Sew into 1 long piece, a little longer than the measurement from Step 1.

3. Refer to the General Instructions (page 44) to measure for the border lengths.

4. Trim the top and bottom borders to the correct length.

5. Sew to the quilt top. Press.

6. Trim the side borders to the correct length.

7. Sew to the quilt top. Press.

## MIDDLE BORDER

Half-Square Triangle Units; make 112.

| FABRIC | SIZE TO CUT | NUMBER TO CUT |
|--------|-------------|---------------|
| Plaids | $2\frac{7}{8}'' \times 2\frac{7}{8}''$ | 56 |
| Black | $2\frac{7}{8}'' \times 2\frac{7}{8}''$ | 56 |

Draw a line.

1. Place a $2\frac{7}{8}''$ plaid square and a $2\frac{7}{8}''$ black square right sides together. Draw a diagonal line.

Stitch.

2. Stitch $\frac{1}{4}''$ from each side of the line.

Cut on the line.

3. Cut on the line and press. Make 112.

**Tip** There are several different products that allow you to make large numbers of half-square triangles without having to cut each one individually. See Resources for these timesavers!

4. Sew 27 units together for each top and bottom border.
5. Stitch to the quilt top. Press.
6. Sew 29 units together for each side border.
7. Stitch to the quilt top. Press.

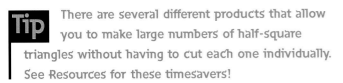

Middle border piecing

## OUTER APPLIQUÉD BORDER

1. Cut 7 strips $10\frac{1}{2}'' \times$ the width of the fabric.
2. Stitch into 1 long length with straight seams.
3. Refer to the General Instructions (page 44) to measure for the border lengths.
4. Trim the top and bottom borders to the correct length.
5. Trim the side borders to the correct length.

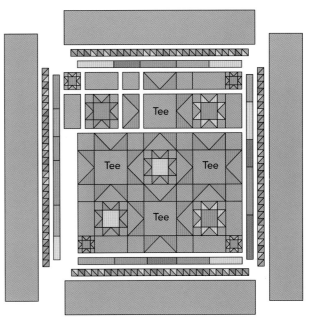

Quilt construction

## VINE FOR OUTER BORDER

1. Cut a square $20'' \times 20''$ from the green fabric. Cut it in half diagonally.

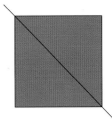

Cut on the diagonal.

2. Place right sides together, as shown, and sew.

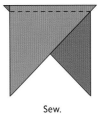

Sew.

3. Press the seam open. On each long bias edge, begin cutting the desired size of strips.

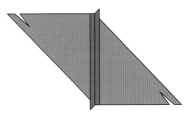

Press the seam open and partially cut the strips.

4. Place the straight-grain edges together to form a tube. Offset the edges by the partially cut strips. Sew and press the seam open.

5. Continue cutting the bias strips from the piece.

Match the opposing edges and sew.

6. **Method 1**: Cut ½˝ bias strips. Feed the strips through a ¼˝ bias tape maker and press.

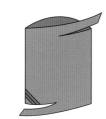

Method 1

**Method 2**: Cut ¾˝ bias strips. Fold and press one edge to the center of the strip. Fold and press the other edge, slightly overlapping the first edge.

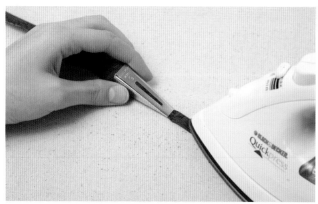

Method 2

**Tip** Place the bias strips in a pile and "toss" with spray starch before you press them. The bias will stay nicely ironed until you're ready to use it.

7. Using a chalk marker, draw curved lines on the border strips. Continue onto each border. These don't have to be perfect; your eye will "fix" the design when it is done.

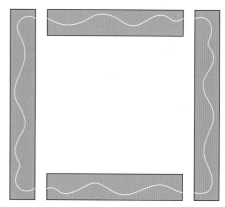

Draw curved lines ending in the corners.

**Tip** Always test your markers for ease of removal.

8. Baste or pin the vine in place. Leave at least 3˝-long tails at the corners. These will be joined after the borders are sewn.

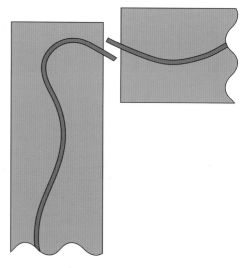

Baste, leaving long tails at the corners.

## FEATHERS FOR OUTER BORDER

1. Trace the pattern on the bottom of this page to make a template for the feathers.
2. Iron the fusible web to the wrong side of a variety of the plaid fabrics.
3. Trace 183 feathers for the inside edge of the vine. Reverse the template and trace 192 feathers for the outside edge of the vine.

Trace the feathers onto fusible web.

> **Tip** You will have right and left feathers; keep them separate in sealable food-storage bags for ease of handling.

4. Cut out the feathers on the marked lines. Arrange them on the border, tucking the ends under the basted vine. Fuse in place following the manufacturer's instructions.

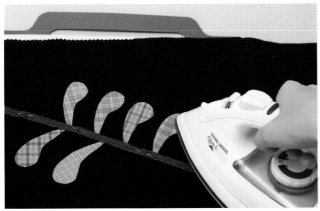

Cut out and fuse in place.

5. Stitch around the feathers and vine with a blanket stitch.

Blanket stitch

6. Stitch the top and bottom borders to the quilt top. Press.
7. Stitch the side borders to the quilt top. Press.
8. Position the ends of the vine and the feathers over the seams. Complete the appliqué.

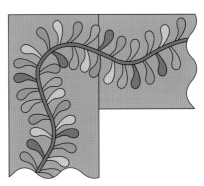

Complete the appliqué.

## finishing

Layer, baste, quilt, bind, and label. I used stippling and echo quilting.

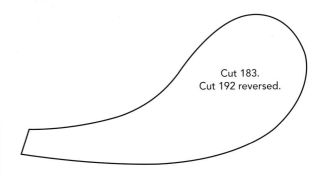

Cut 183.
Cut 192 reversed.

# RELAY FOR LIFE

*This project will work for any heartfelt theme. The heart blocks were designed by Diana McClun and Laura Nownes for their book, **Say It With Quilts**. I used several different pink and purple fabrics that complemented the colors in my T-shirts for the heart blocks. This makes a nice scrappy quilt.*

Finished quilt: 61½″ × 85″
FINISHED BLOCK SIZES:
Small Hearts: 4½″ × 4″
Medium Hearts: 6″ × 6″
Large Hearts: 12″ × 12″

# materials

*Based on 42˝ fabric width.*

- Assorted pink and purple prints: 3 yards total for heart blocks
- White: 2 yards for background
- Purple print: 1⅛ yards for sashing
- Dark purple: ½ yard for inner border
- Print: 1¾ yards for outer border
- Backing: 5¼ yards
- Batting: 66˝ × 89˝
- Binding: ¾ yard
- Lightweight fusible interfacing: 2¾ yards

# cutting

Small Heart Blocks: 4½˝ × 4˝; make 18 (reverse fabric placement for 6).

| FABRIC | SIZE TO CUT | NUMBER TO CUT (PER BLOCK) |
|---|---|---|
| Prints | 2¾˝ × 2¼˝ | 2 |
| Prints | 3⅛˝ × 3⅛˝ | 1 |
| White | 1˝ × 1˝ | 4 |
| White | 3⅛˝ × 3⅛˝ | 1 |

Medium Heart Blocks (Quartered): 6˝ × 6˝; make 12.

| FABRIC | SIZE TO CUT | NUMBER TO CUT (PER PAIR OF BLOCKS) |
|---|---|---|
| Prints | 3½˝ × 3½˝ | 4 |
| Prints | 3⅞˝ × 3⅞˝ | 2 |
| White | 1½˝ × 1½˝ | 8 |
| White | 3⅞˝ × 3⅞˝ | 2 |

Medium Heart Blocks (Striped): 6˝ × 6˝; make 12.

| FABRIC | SIZE TO CUT | NUMBER TO CUT (PER BLOCK) |
|---|---|---|
| Prints | 1½˝ × 3½˝ | 6 |
| Prints | 3⅞˝ × 3⅞˝ | 1 |
| White | 1½˝ × 1½˝ | 4 |
| White | 3⅞˝ × 3⅞˝ | 1 |

Large Heart Blocks: 12˝ × 12˝; make 6.

| FABRIC | SIZE TO CUT | NUMBER TO CUT (PER BLOCK) |
|---|---|---|
| Prints | 2½˝ × 6½˝ | 6 |
| Prints | 6⅞˝ × 6⅞˝ | 1 |
| White | 2½˝ × 2½˝ | 4 |
| White | 6⅞˝ × 6⅞˝ | 1 |

# construction

*Use a ¼˝ seam allowance.*

Prepare the shirts (pages 25–26) and trim to 12⅝˝ × 12⅝˝. Make 6.

## SMALL AND MEDIUM HEARTS

*Instructions are for 1 heart block.*

1. For the small blocks, place 2 of the 1˝ white squares on the corners of a 2¾˝ × 2¼˝ print rectangle (oriented horizontally). For the medium blocks, place 2 of the 1½˝ squares on the corners of a 3½˝ print square. Draw a line and stitch from corner to corner. Trim and press open. Make 2 for each heart block.

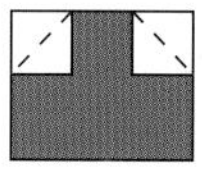

Make 2.

2. For the small blocks, place a 3⅛˝ print square and a 3⅛˝ white square right sides together. For the medium blocks, place a 3⅞˝ print square and a 3⅞˝ white square right sides together. Draw a diagonal line.

3. Stitch ¼˝ from each side of the line.

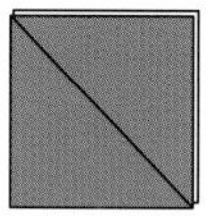

Draw a line. 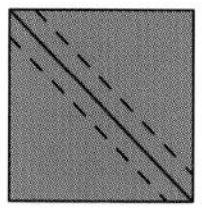          Stitch.

4. Cut on the line and press. Make 2 for each heart block.

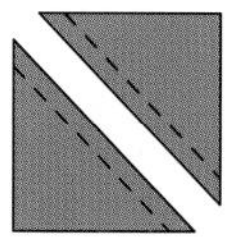

Cut on the line.

5. Arrange the units. Stitch and press.

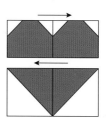

Arrange, stitch, and press.

## STRIPED HEARTS

*Instructions are for 1 heart block. Arrows indicate pressing direction.*

1. For the medium blocks, stitch 3 print rectangles $1\frac{1}{2}'' \times 3\frac{1}{2}''$ together. For the large heart block, stitch 3 print rectangles $2\frac{1}{2}'' \times 6\frac{1}{2}''$ together. Make 2 for each block.

Stitch.

2. Press the units for each block in opposite directions.

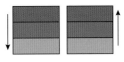

Press.

3. For the medium blocks, place 2 of the $1\frac{1}{2}''$ white squares on the corners of the units. For the large blocks, place 2 of the $2\frac{1}{2}''$ white squares on the corners of the units. Draw a line and stitch from corner to corner. Trim and press open. Make 2 for each block.

Make 2.

4. For the medium blocks, place a $3\frac{7}{8}''$ print square and a $3\frac{7}{8}''$ white square right sides together. For the large blocks, place a $6\frac{7}{8}''$ print square and a $6\frac{7}{8}''$ white square right sides together. Draw a diagonal line.

Draw a line.

5. Stitch $\frac{1}{4}''$ from each side of the line.

Stitch.

6. Cut on the line and press. Make 2 for each heart block.

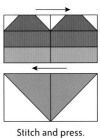

Cut on the line.

7. Arrange the units. Stitch and press.

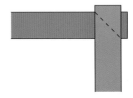

Stitch and press.

# assembling the quilt top

1. Position the blocks and tees in vertical rows, referring to the quilt construction diagram.
2. Sew into vertical rows. Press.
3. Cut 8 strips $2\frac{1}{2}'' \times$ the length of the fabric for the sashing pieces.
4. Stitch pairs of strips together with diagonal seams. Trim and press open.

Stitch with diagonal seams.

Press.

5. Measure the rows to determine the length of the sashing pieces. Trim the pieces to the correct length.
6. Sew the rows and sashing pieces together. Press.

## INNER BORDER

1. Cut 8 strips 1½″ × the width of the fabric.
2. Stitch into 1 long length with diagonal seams.
3. Refer to the General Instructions (page 44) for how to measure your quilt for borders.
4. Trim the top and bottom borders to the correct length.
5. Sew to the quilt top. Press.
6. Trim the side borders to the correct length.
7. Sew to the quilt top. Press.

## OUTER BORDER

1. Cut 8 strips 6″ × the width of the fabric.
2. Stitch into 1 long length with diagonal seams (page 34).
3. Refer to the General Instructions (page 44) for how to measure your quilt for borders.
4. Trim the side borders to the correct length.
5. Sew to the quilt top. Press.
6. Trim the top and bottom borders to the correct length.
7. Sew to the quilt top. Press.

## finishing

Layer, baste, quilt, bind, and label. I machine quilted using a heart-shaped quilting template in the small hearts and free-motion quilted in the large hearts.

Quilt construction

# 3RD OF JULY

*In real estate sales we work very hard, and in my office we play just as hard! In the 3rd of July Torchlight Parade in Benicia, California, our kazoo band is legendary. So are our tees. This quilt design would also work for just about any other theme. Let your imagination go wild.*

Finished quilt: 66″ × 66″
FINISHED BLOCK SIZE:
12″ × 12″

## materials

*Based on 42˝ fabric width.*

- Assorted reds: 2¾ yards total for blocks, sashing, and border
- Assorted whites: 2½ yards total for blocks, sashing, and border
- Blue: 1⅛ yard for sashing and border
- Backing: 4¼ yards
- Batting: 70˝ × 70˝
- Binding: ¾ yard
- Lightweight fusible interfacing: 2¾ yards

## cutting

Log Cabin Blocks: 12˝ × 12˝; make 10.

| FABRIC | SIZE TO CUT | NUMBER TO CUT |
|---|---|---|
| Red | 2˝ × width of fabric | 17 strips |
| White | 2˝ × width of fabric | 20 strips |
| Red | 3½˝ × 3½˝ | 10 |

Sashing

| FABRIC | SIZE TO CUT | NUMBER TO CUT |
|---|---|---|
| Red | 2˝ × 12½˝ | 40 |
| White | 2˝ × 12½˝ | 40 |
| Blue | 2˝ × 2˝ | 160 |
| Blue | 3½˝ × 3½˝ | 25 |

Border

| FABRIC | SIZE TO CUT | NUMBER TO CUT |
|---|---|---|
| Red | 2˝ × 3½˝ | 10 |
| Red | 2˝ × 2˝ | 2 |
| Red | 2˝ × 12½˝ | 8 |
| White | 2˝ × 3½˝ | 10 |
| White | 2˝ × 2˝ | 2 |
| White | 2˝ × 12½˝ | 8 |
| Blue | 2˝ × 2˝ | 40 |

## construction

*Use a ¼˝ seam allowance.*

Prepare the shirts (pages 25–26) and trim to 12⅝˝ × 12⅝˝. Make 6. If desired, prepare a small motif to use in the sashing instead of a blue square. Trim to 3⅝˝ × 3⅝˝.

### LOG CABIN BLOCKS

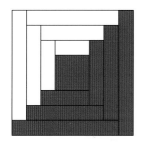

Log Cabin block

1. Use strip-piecing techniques to make the Log Cabin blocks. Place the 3½˝ red squares on white strips and stitch. Cut apart the units and press.

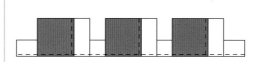 

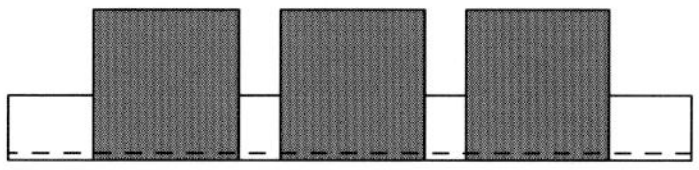

Stitch the center to the strip. 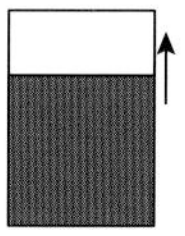  Cut apart and press.

2. Pivot the units and place them on white strips again and stitch. Cut apart and press.

Add the next strip.  Cut apart and press.

3. Pivot the units and place them on red strips and stitch. Cut apart and press.

Add the next strip.  Cut apart and press.

4. Pivot the units and place them on red strips again and stitch. Cut apart and press.

Add the next strip.

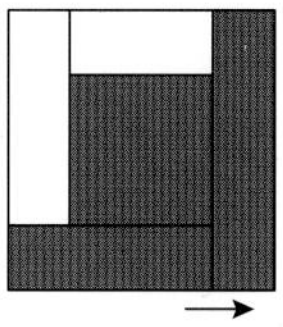

Cut apart and press. One row of strips around the center square is complete.

5. Continue stitching the units to the strips, using each color twice before switching to the other color. Sew 3 complete rows of strips around the center square. Make 10 blocks.

 I used Marti Michell's Log Cabin ruler for fast and accurate piecing (see Resources on page 46).

## SASHING

1. Draw a diagonal line on the back of 2 of the 2″ blue squares. Place the squares on the ends of a 2″ × 12½″ red or white rectangle.

Draw a line and place on the rectangle.

2. Stitch on the line from corner to corner.

Stitch.

3. Trim and press. Make 40 units with red rectangles and 40 with white rectangles.

Press.

4. Stitch the units together in pairs, referring to the quilt construction diagram.

> Instead of marking all the pieces, mark the bed of your sewing machine. Create a line by placing masking tape so the edge is exactly in front of the needle. For a perfect triangle, keep the corner of the square on the line while you are stitching.

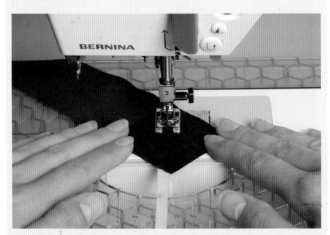

Keep the corner on the line while stitching.

## BORDER

1. Place a 2″ blue square on a 2″ × 3½″ red or white rectangle. Draw a line and sew from corner to corner.

Stitch.

2. Trim the excess fabric and press.

Press.

3. Repeat for the other end. Make 10 units with red rectangles and 10 units with white rectangles.

Repeat.

## assembling the quilt top

Position and stitch the blocks, tees, sashing, and border pieces, referring to the quilt construction diagram. Press.

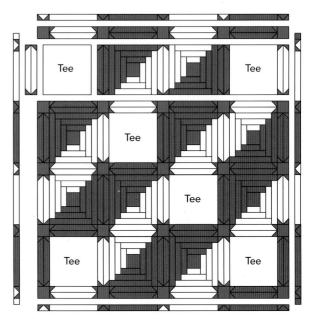

Quilt construction

## finishing

Layer, baste, quilt, bind, and label. One of my favorite things about these quilts is that very little quilting is needed. In this quilt, I used simple stitch-in-the-ditch quilting.

# GO BEARS

*This project really illustrates how to let your tees design the quilt. The University of California at Berkeley's football team is the Golden Bears. So, what better quilt block to use than a traditional Bear's Paw? However, it could just as easily have been a cat paw, wolf paw, or any other animal track.*

Finished quilt: 58″ × 58″
FINISHED BLOCK SIZE:
14″ × 14″

## materials

*Based on 42˝ fabric width.*

- Gold: ¾ yard for blocks and sashing
- Dark gold: ½ yard for blocks
- Dark blue: ¾ yard for background
- Brown: ½ yard for inner border
- Dark blue print: 1¾ yards for outer border
- Backing: 3¾ yards
- Batting: 62˝ × 62˝
- Binding: ⅝ yard
- Lightweight fusible interfacing: 2½ yards

## cutting

Bear's Paw block: 14˝ × 14˝; make 4.

| FABRIC | SIZE TO CUT | NUMBER TO CUT (PER BLOCK) |
|--------|-------------|---------------------------|
| Gold | 2⅞˝ × 2⅞˝ | 8 |
| Gold | 2½˝ × 2½˝ | 1 |
| Dark gold | 4½˝ × 4½˝ | 4 |
| Dark blue | 2⅞˝ × 2⅞˝ | 8 |
| Dark blue | 2½˝ × 2½˝ | 4 |
| Dark blue | 2½˝ × 6½˝ | 4 |

 **Note** The triangles, or claws on the paws, are directional.

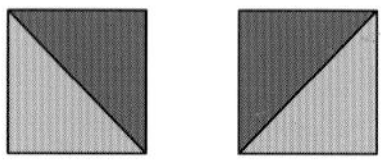

## construction

*Use a ¼˝ seam allowance.*

Prepare the shirts (pages 25–26) and trim to 14⅝˝ × 14⅝˝. Make 5.

### BEAR'S PAW BLOCKS

Instructions are for 1 block.

1. Place a 2⅞˝ gold square and a 2⅞˝ dark blue square right sides together. Draw a diagonal line.

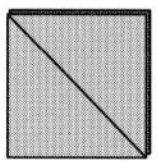

Draw a line.

2. Stitch ¼˝ from each side of the line.

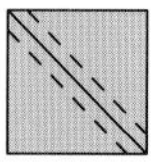

Stitch.

3. Cut on the line and press. Make 16.

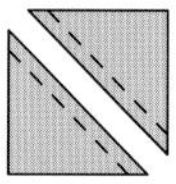

Cut on the line.

4. Arrange the units with the 4½˝ dark gold squares and the 2½˝ dark blue squares. Stitch and press. Make 4.

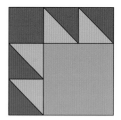

Make 4.

5. Arrange the units with the 2½˝ gold squares and the dark blue rectangles. Stitch and press. Make 4 blocks.

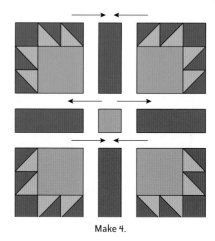

Make 4.

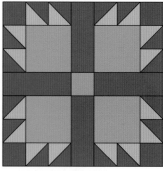

Bear's Paw block

## assembling the quilt top

1. Cut 5 strips 1″ × the width of the fabric for the sashing pieces.
2. Stitch the strips together with diagonal seams.
3. Cut into 6 pieces 1″ × 14½″ and 2 pieces 1″ × 43½″.
4. Position and stitch the blocks, tees, and sashing pieces, referring to the quilt construction diagram.

### INNER BORDER

1. Cut 5 strips 2″ × the width of the fabric.
2. Stitch into 1 long length with diagonal seams (page 34).
3. Refer to the General Instructions (page 44) for how to measure your quilt for borders.
4. Trim the side borders to the correct length.
5. Sew to the quilt top. Press.
6. Trim the top and bottom borders to the correct length.
7. Sew to the quilt top. Press.

### OUTER BORDER

1. Cut 7 strips 6½″ × the width of the fabric.
2. Stitch into 1 long length with diagonal seams (page 34).
3. Refer to the General Instructions (page 44) for how to measure your quilt for borders.
4. Trim the side borders to the correct length.
5. Sew to the quilt top. Press.
6. Trim the top and bottom borders to the correct length.
7. Sew to the quilt top. Press.

## finishing

Layer, baste, quilt, bind, and label. I quilted in the ditch around the blocks and around the motifs.

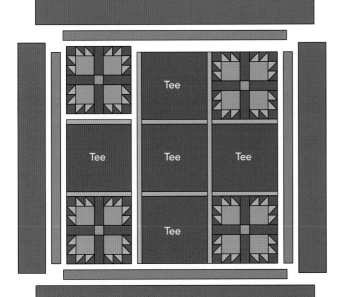

Quilt construction

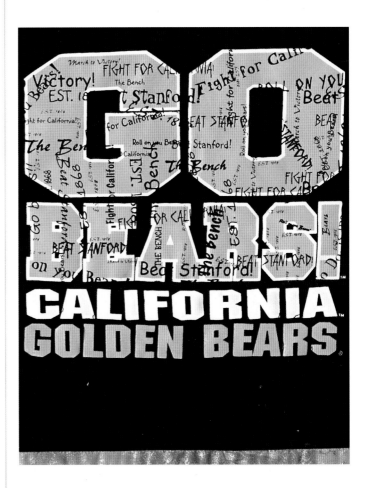

As with all quilting projects, these quilts require some tools and supplies. There are some must-haves and a few good-to-haves. Some of these you will already own and some you will want to add to your sewing room.

First and foremost, you need a sewing machine in good working order—cleaned and oiled, with a new needle. The tees can be difficult to work with, and a walking foot can help.

Bernina 660, needles, oil, and assorted feet (including a walking foot)

You will need a rotary cutter, mat, and acrylic rulers in various sizes. If you are working with large motifs in your tees, a large square ruler can be a great help.

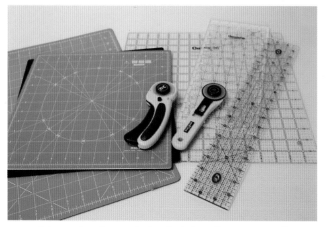

Rotary mats, cutters, and rulers (including a large square one)

Threads! You need beautiful, good-quality threads for piecing and for quilting.

Variety of threads

Use fine glass-headed pins. Flat flower-head pins can come in handy, too. Nice long-bladed scissors and a sharp seam ripper are must-haves. A gridded pressing surface is very handy.

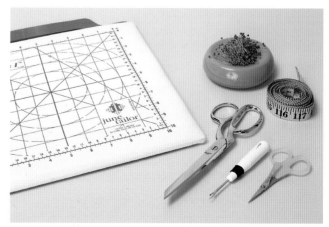

Seam ripper, scissors, pins and gridded pressing surface

There are a few more must-haves for creating a successful T-shirt quilt: fusible adhesive, a nonstick pressing sheet, and cleaner for removing fusible adhesive from your iron. Accidents do happen, and this stuff works well. And, of course, you need a good working iron.

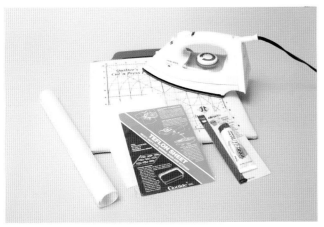

Pressing sheet, glue remover, iron, and pressing surface

An absolute must-have is fusible nonwoven interfacing. There are many brands and weights, but a light to medium weight interfacing works best. It is available in precut lengths or by the yard off the bolt.

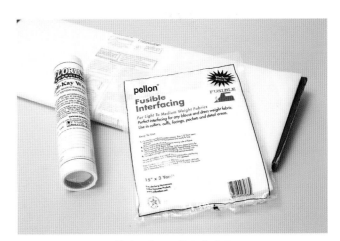

Various types of interfacing

## measuring for borders

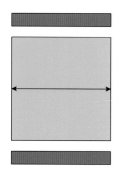

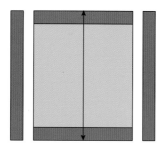

Measure through the center from side to side for the top and bottom borders.

Measure through the center from top to bottom for the side borders.

## finishing your quilt

### BACKING

Make the backing a minimum of 3˝ larger than the quilt top on all sides. Prewash the fabric, and trim the selvages before you piece.

### BATTING

The choice of batting to use is a personal decision; consult your local quilt shop. Cut the batting approximately 3˝ larger on all sides than your quilt top.

### LAYERING

1. Spread the backing wrong side up and tape the edges down with masking tape. (If you are working on carpet you can use T-pins to secure the backing to the carpet.)
2. Center the batting on top, smoothing out any folds.
3. Place the quilt top right side up on top of the batting and backing, making sure it's centered.

### BASTING

Baste the layers with a needle and thread or with small safety pins. If you pin baste, do not pin through the ink areas on the tees, as the pins may leave holes.

### QUILTING

The instructions for each quilt project indicate how the quilt was quilted. Do any intricate quilting on the pieced blocks; the tee blocks get simple quilting and stippling. The tee blocks are a puffy area in your quilt and do not take well to quilting. Thick ink will fight with your machine. After making many of these quilts, I have decided to let the ink win. I try not to quilt through those areas. Instead, I quilt as close as possible to the images. If there are open areas—nonprinted areas within the motif—I quilt those areas as well. On some tees, the ink is thin and doesn't create any problems. If you have some of these, hooray! Your quilting just got easier. Don't forget that you are quilting through the interfacing as well.

Stippling on fused material

**Tip** Remember the sample you tested for fusibility (page 26)? Test your quilting thread and needle selection on that.

## DOUBLE-FOLD STRAIGHT-GRAIN BINDING (FRENCH FOLD)

1. Trim the excess batting and backing from the quilt. If you want a ¼″ finished binding, cut the strips 2″ wide and piece them together with a diagonal seam to make a continuous binding strip.

2. Press the seams open, then press the entire strip in half lengthwise with wrong sides together. With raw edges even, pin the binding to the edge of the quilt a few inches away from the corner, and leave the first few inches of the binding unattached. Start sewing, using a ¼″ seam allowance.

3. Stop ¼″ away from the first corner and backstitch one stitch.

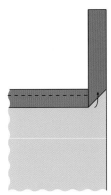

¼″ from corner

Stitch to ¼″ from the corner.

4. Lift the presser foot and needle. Rotate the quilt 90°. Fold the binding up at a right angle so it extends straight above the quilt, forming a 45° fold in the corner of the binding.

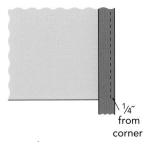

First fold for the miter

5. Then bring the binding strip down even with the edge of the quilt. Begin sewing at the folded edge.

Second fold alignment. Repeat in the same manner at all corners.

### FINISHING THE BINDING

**Method 1:**
Fold under the beginning end of the binding strip ¼″. Lay the ending binding strip over the beginning folded end. Continue stitching beyond the folded edge. Trim the excess binding. Fold the binding over the raw edges to the quilt back and hand stitch, mitering the corners.

**Method 2:**
Fold the ending tail of the binding back on itself where it meets the beginning binding tail. From the fold, measure and mark the cut width of the binding strip. Cut the ending binding tail to this measurement. For example, if the binding is cut 2¼″ wide, measure from the fold on the ending tail of the binding 2¼″ and cut the binding tail to this length.

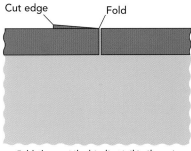

Cut edge          Fold

Fold, then cut the binding tail to the cut width of the binding.

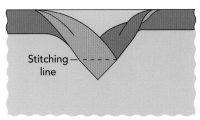

Stitching line

Stitch the ends of the binding diagonally.

Open both tails. Place one tail on top of the other tail at right angles, right sides together. Mark a diagonal line and stitch on the line. Trim the seam to ¼″. Press open.

## LABELING

These quilts are very special, so be sure to label them. Include whose shirts were used, who made the quilt, and any other interesting tidbits. The more information, the better.

# Resources

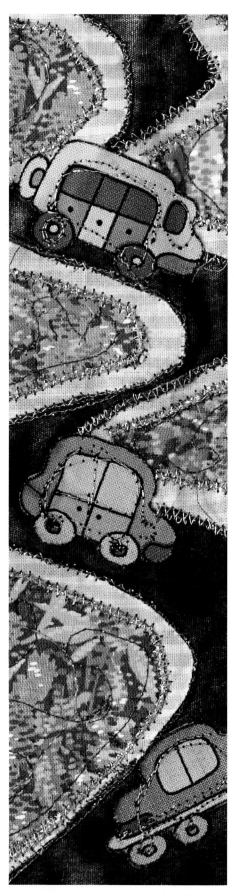

**CATALOG OF BOOKS AND PRODUCTS:**

C&T Publishing
P.O. Box 1456
Lafayette, CA 94549
(800) 284-1114
email: ctinfo@ctpub.com
website: www.ctpub.com

**QUILTING SUPPLIES:**

COTTON PATCH
1025 Brown Ave.
Lafayette, CA 94549
(800) 835-4418 or
(925) 283-7883
email: CottonPa@aol.com
website: www.quiltusa.com

PATCHWORK CAT
940 Tyler #16
Benicia, CA 94510
(707) 748-7541
website: www.patchworkcat.com

MARTI MICHELL
Log Cabin Ruler
P.O. Box 80218
Atlanta, GA 30366
(800) 558-3568
website: www.frommarti.com

QUILTIME
Triangle paper
7103 Wolf Rivers Avenue
Las Vegas, NV 89131
(702) 658-7988
website: www.quiltime.com

**PHOTOGRAPHY SERVICES:**

www.ctmediaservices.com

**BOOKS:**

*Setting Solutions* by Sharyn Craig (C&T Publishing)
*Great Sets* by Sharyn Craig (C&T Publishing)
*Smashing Sets* by Margaret Miller (C&T Publishing)
*Quick & Easy Block Tool* (C&T Publishing)

# About the Author

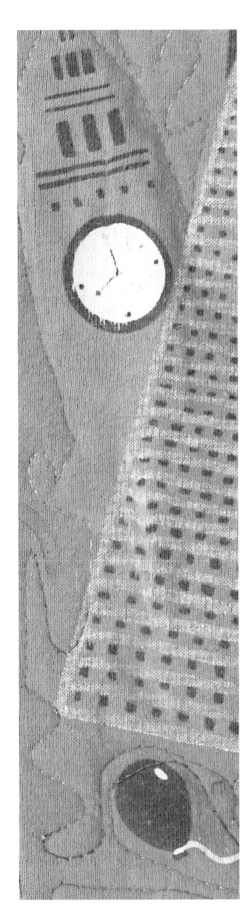

Roberta De Luz has been stitching since she could hold a needle. She studied industrial arts at the College of the Alameda, supporting herself by doing alterations and selling handmade clothes. However, she did not start quilting until 1990, when she was taken to a quilt shop on a date.

She is passionate about the process of quiltmaking, concentrating on the details of design and execution. This passion has led several of her quilts to travel in national exhibits for Quilts for a Cure (2002), the Hoffman Challenge (2004), and the Kaufman Challenge (2005). She loves her quilts to be used and does her best work when the quilts have a purpose.

The choice of designing T-shirt quilts was totally serendipitous. "I think if the first one had been anything other than *Bay to Breakers*, I might not have made the leap in this direction. The tees were so inspiring—it just happened."

Roberta is a realtor when she isn't sewing in her Benicia, California, home, which she shares with two cats. She is the mother of one grown son, Tony, and grandmother to Arianna.

# Great Titles

## from

### C&T PUBLISHING

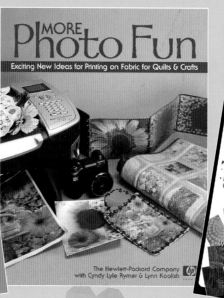

## Available at your local retailer or
# www.ctpub.com or 800.284.1114